Kristen Suzanne's
EASY
Raw Vegan
Salads &
Dressings

Fun & Easy Raw Food Recipes for
Making the World's Most Delicious
& Healthy Salads for Yourself,
Your Family & Entertaining

by Kristen Suzanne

Green
Butterfly
Press

Scottsdale, Arizor

D0841368

OTHER BOOKS BY KRISTEN SUZANNE

- *Kristen's Raw: The EASY Way to Get Started & Succeed at the Raw Food Vegan Diet & Lifestyle*
- *Kristen Suzanne's EASY Raw Vegan Entrees*
- *Kristen Suzanne's EASY Raw Vegan Desserts*
- *Kristen Suzanne's EASY Raw Vegan Soups*
- *Kristen Suzanne's EASY Raw Vegan Sides & Snacks*
- *Kristen Suzanne's EASY Raw Vegan Smoothies, Juices, Elixirs & Drinks (includes wine drinks!)*
- *Kristen Suzanne's EASY Raw Vegan Holidays*
- *Kristen Suzanne's EASY Raw Vegan Dehydrating*
- *Kristen Suzanne's Ultimate Raw Vegan Hemp Recipes*

COMING SOON

- *Kristen Suzanne's Raw Vegan Diet for EASY Weight Loss*
- *Kristen Suzanne's Ultimate Raw Vegan Chocolate Recipes*

For details, Raw Food resources, and Kristen's free Raw Food newsletter, please visit:

KristensRaw.com

For information on excerpting, reprinting or licensing portions of this book, please write to info@greenbutterflypress.com.

Green Butterfly Press
19550 N. Gray Hawk Drive, Suite 1042
Scottsdale, AZ 85255 USA

Library of Congress Control Number: 2008943619
Library of Congress Subject Heading:
1. Cookery (Natural foods) 2. Raw foods

ISBN: 978-0-9817556-6-3
1.1

CONTENTS

CHAPTER 1

RAW BASICS

NOTE: "Raw Basics" is a brief introduction to Raw for those who are new to the subject. It is the same in all of my recipe books. If you have recently read this section in one of them, you may wish to skip to Chapter 2.

WHY RAW?

Living the Raw vegan lifestyle has made me a more effective person... in everything I do. I get to experience pure, sustainable all-day-long energy. My body is in perfect shape and I gain strength and endurance in my exercise routine with each passing day. My relationships are the best they've ever been, because I'm happy and I love myself and my life. My headaches have ceased to exist, and my skin glows with the radiance of brand new life, which is exactly how I feel. Raw vegan is the best thing that has ever happened to me.

Whatever your passion is in life (family, business, exercise, meditation, hobbies, etc.), eating Raw vegan will take it to unbelievable new heights. Raw vegan food offers you the most amazing benefits – physically, mentally, and spiritually. It is *the* ideal choice for your food consumption if you want to become the healthiest and best "you" possible. Raw vegan food is for people who want to live longer while feeling younger. It's for people who want to feel vibrant and alive, and want to enjoy life like never before. All I ever have to say to someone is, "Just try it for yourself." It will change your life. From simple to gourmet, there's always something for everyone, and it's delicious. Come into the world of Raw with me, and experience for yourself the most amazing health *ever*.

Are you ready for your new lease on life? The time is now. Let's get started!

SOME GREAT THINGS TO KNOW BEFORE DIVING INTO THESE RECIPES

Organic Food

I use organic produce and products for pretty much everything. There are very few exceptions, and that would be if the recipe called for something I just can't get organic such as jicama, young Thai coconuts, certain seasonings, or any random ingredient that my local health food store is not able to procure from an organic grower for whatever reason.

If you think organic foods are too expensive, then start in baby steps and buy a few things at a time. Realize that you're going to be spending less money in the long run on health problems as your health improves, and going organic is one way to facilitate that. I find that once people learn about the direct cause-and-effect relationship between non-organic food and illnesses such as cancer, the relatively small premium you pay for organic becomes a trivial non-issue. Your health is worth it!

Choosing organically grown foods is one of the most important choices we can make. The more people who choose organic, the lower the prices will be in the long run. Vote with your dollar! Here is something I do to help further this cause and you can, too… whenever I eat at a restaurant I always write on the bill, "I would eat here more if you served organic food." Can you imagine what would happen if we all did this?

It's essential to use organic ingredients for many reasons:

1. The health benefits – superior nutrition, reduced intake of chemicals and heavy metals and decreased exposure to carcinogens. Organic food has been shown to have up to 300% more nutrition than conventionally grown, non-organic produce.

2. To have the very best tasting food ever! I've had people tell me in my classes that they never knew vegetables tasted so good – and it's because I only use organic.

3. Greater variety of heirloom fruits and vegetables.

4. Cleaner rivers and waterways for our earth, along with minimized topsoil erosion.

Going Organic on a Budget:

Going organic on a budget is not impossible. Here are things to keep in mind that will help you afford it:

1. Buy in bulk. Ask the store you frequent if they'll give you a deal for buying certain foods by the case. (Just make sure it's a case of something that you can go through in a timely fashion so it doesn't go to waste). Consider this for bananas or greens especially if you drink lots of smoothies or green juice, like I do.

2. See if local neighbors, family or friends will share the price of getting cases of certain foods. When you do this, you can go beyond your local grocery store and contact great places (which deliver nationally) such as Boxed Greens (BoxedGreens.com) or Diamond Organics (DiamondOrganics.com). Maybe they'll extend a discount if your order goes above a certain

amount or if you get certain foods by the case. It never hurts to ask.

3. Pay attention to organic foods that are not very expensive to buy relative to the conventional prices (bananas, for example). Load up on those.

4. Be smart when picking what you buy as organic. Some conventionally grown foods have higher levels of pesticides than others. For those, go organic. Then, for foods that are not sprayed as much, you can go conventional. Avocados, for example, aren't sprayed too heavily so you could buy those as conventional. Here is a resource that keeps an updated list:

5. foodnews.org/walletguide.php

6. Buy produce that is on sale. Pay attention to which organic foods are on sale for the week and plan your menu around that. Every little bit adds up!

7. Grow your own sprouts. Load up on these for salads, soups, and smoothies. Very inexpensive. Buy the organic seeds in the bulk bins at your health food store or buy online and grow them yourself. Fun!

8. Buy organic seeds/nuts in bulk online and freeze. Nuts and seeds typically get less expensive when you order in bulk from somewhere like Sun Organic (SunOrganic.com). Take advantage of this and freeze them (they'll last the year!). Do the same with dried fruits/dates/etc. And remember, when you make a recipe that calls for expensive nuts, you can often easily replace them with a less expensive seed such as sunflower or pumpkin seeds.

9. Buy seasonally; hence, don't buy a bunch of organic berries out of season (i.e., eat more apples and bananas in the fall and winter). Also, consider buying frozen organic fruits, especially when they're on sale!

10. Be content with minimal variety. Organic spinach banana smoothies are inexpensive. So, having this most mornings for your breakfast can save you money. You can change it up for fun by adding cinnamon one day, nutmeg another, vanilla extract yet another. Another inexpensive meal or snack is a spinach apple smoothie. Throw in a date or some raisins for extra pizazz. It helps the budget when you make salads, smoothies, and soups with ingredients that tend to be less expensive such as carrots (year round), bananas (year round), zucchini and cucumbers (in the summer), etc.

Kristen Suzanne's Tip: A Note About Herbs

Hands down, fresh herbs taste the best and have the highest nutritional value. While I recommend fresh herbs whenever possible, you can substitute dried herbs if necessary. But do so in a ratio of:

3 parts fresh to 1 part dried

Dried herbs impart a more concentrated flavor, which is why you need less of them. For instance, if your recipe calls for three tablespoons of fresh basil, you'll be fine if you use one tablespoon of dried basil instead.

The Infamous Salt Question: What Kind Do I Use?

All life on earth began in the oceans, so it's no surprise that organisms' cellular fluids chemically resemble sea water. Saltwater in the ocean is "salty" due to many, many minerals, not just sodium chloride. We need these minerals, not coincidentally, in roughly the same proportion that they exist in... guess where?... the ocean! (You've just gotta love Mother Nature.)

So when preparing food, I always use sea salt, which can be found at any health food store. Better still is sea salt that was deposited into salt beds before the industrial revolution started spewing toxins into the world's waterways. My personal preference is Himalayan Crystal Salt, fine granules. It's mined high in the mountains from ancient sea-beds, has a beautiful pink color, and imparts more than 84 essential minerals into your diet. You can use either the Himalayan crystal variety or Celtic Sea Salt, but I would highly recommend sticking to at least one of these two. You can buy Himalayan crystal salt through KristensRaw.com/store.

Kristen Suzanne's Tip: Start Small with Strong Flavors

FLAVORS AND THEIR STRENGTH

There are certain flavors and ingredients that are particularly strong, such as garlic, ginger, onion, and salt. It's important to observe patience here, as these are flavors that can be loved or considered offensive, depending on who is eating the food. I know people who want the maximum amount of salt called for in a recipe and I know some who are highly sensitive to it. Therefore, to make the best possible Raw experience for you, I recommend starting on the "small end" especially with ingredients like garlic, ginger, strong savory herbs and seasonings, onions (any variety), citrus, and even salt. If I've given you a range in a recipe, for instance *1/4 - 1/2 teaspoon Himalayan crystal salt* then I recommend starting with the smaller amount, and then tasting it. If you don't love it, then add a little more of that ingredient and taste it again. Start small. It's worth the extra 60 seconds it might take you to do this. You might end up using less, saving it for the next recipe you make and voila, you're saving a little money.

Lesson #1: It's very hard to correct any flavors of excess, so start small and build.

Lesson #2: Write it down. When an ingredient offers a "range" for itself, write down the amount you liked best. If you use an "optional" ingredient, make a note about that as well.

One more thing to know about some strong flavors like the ones mentioned above... with Raw food, these flavors can intensify the finished product as each day passes. For example, the garlic in your soup, on the day you made it, might be perfect. On day two, it's still really great but a little stronger in flavor. And by day three, you might want to carry around your toothbrush or a little chewing gum!

HERE IS A TIP TO HELP CONTROL THIS

If you're making a recipe in advance, such as a dressing or soup that you won't be eating until the following day or even the day after that, then hold off on adding some of the strong seasonings until the day you eat it (think garlic and ginger). Or, if you're going to make the dressing or soup in advance, use less of the strong seasoning, knowing that it might intensify on its own by the time you eat it. This isn't a huge deal because it doesn't change that dramatically, but I mention it so you won't be surprised, especially when serving a favorite dish to others.

Kristen Suzanne's Tip: Doubling Recipes

More often than not, there are certain ingredients and flavors that you don't typically double in their entirety, if you're making a double or triple batch of a recipe. These are strong-flavored ingredients similar to those mentioned above (salt, garlic, ginger, herbs, seasoning, etc). A good rule of thumb is this: For a double batch, use 1.5 times the amount for certain ingredients. Taste it and see if you need the rest. For instance, if I'm making a "double batch" of soup, and the normal recipe calls for 1 tablespoon of Himalayan crystal salt, then I'll put in 1 1/2 tablespoons to start, instead of two. Then, I'll taste it and add the remaining 1/2 tablespoon, if necessary.

This same principle is not necessarily followed when dividing a recipe in half. Go ahead and simply divide in half, or by whatever amount you're making. If there is a range for a particular ingredient provided, I still recommend that you use the smaller amount of an ingredient when dividing. Taste the final product and then decide whether or not to add more.

My recipes provide a variety of yields, as you'll see below. Some recipes make 2 servings and some make 4 - 6 servings. For those of you making food for only yourself, then simply cut the recipes making 4 - 6 servings in half. Or, as I always do... I make the larger serving size and then I have enough food for a couple of meals. If a recipe yields 2 servings, I usually double it for the same reason.

Kristen Suzanne's Tip: Changing Produce

"But I made it exactly like this last time! Why doesn't it taste the same?"

Here is something you need to embrace when preparing Raw vegan food. Fresh produce can vary in its composition of water, and even flavor, to some degree. There are times I've made marinara sauce and, to me, it was the perfect level of sweetness in the finished product. Then, the next time I made it, you would have thought I added a smidge of sweetener. This is due to the fact that fresh Raw produce can have a slightly different taste from time to time when you make a recipe (only ever so slightly, so don't be alarmed). *Aahhh, here is the silver lining!* This means you'll never get bored living the Raw vegan lifestyle because your recipes can change a little in flavor from time to time, even though you followed the same recipe. Embrace this natural aspect of produce and love it for everything that it is. ☺

This is much less of an issue with cooked food. Most of the water is taken out of cooked food, so you typically get the same flavors and experience each and every time. Boring!

Kristen Suzanne's Tip: Ripeness and Storage for Your Fresh Produce

1. I never use green bell peppers because they are not "ripe." This is why so many people have a hard time digesting them (often "belching" after eating them). To truly experience the greatest health, it's important to eat fruits and vegetables at their peak ripeness. Therefore, make sure you only use red, orange, or yellow bell peppers. Store these in your refrigerator.

2. A truly ripe banana has some brown freckles or spots on the peel. This is when you're supposed to eat a banana. Store these on your countertop away from other produce, because bananas give off a gas as they ripen, which will affect the ripening process of your other produce. And, if you have a lot of bananas, split them up. This will help prevent all of your bananas from ripening at once.

3. Keep avocados on the counter until they reach ripeness (when their skin is usually brown in color and if you gently squeeze it, it "gives" just a little). At this point, you can put them in the refrigerator where they'll last up to a week longer. If you keep ripe avocados on the counter, they'll only last another couple of days. Avocados, like bananas, give off a gas as they ripen, which will affect the ripening process of your other produce. Let them ripen away from your other produce. And, if you have a lot of avocados, separate them. This will help prevent all of your avocados from ripening at once.

4. Tomatoes are best stored on your counter. Do not put them in the refrigerator or they'll get a "mealy" texture.

5. Pineapple is ripe for eating when you can gently pull a leaf out of the top of it. Therefore, test your pineapple for ripeness at the store to ensure you're buying the sweetest one possible. Just pull one of the leaves out from the top. After 3 to 4 attempts on different leaves, if you can't gently take one of them out, then move on to another pineapple.

6. Stone fruits (fruits with pits, such as peaches, plums, and nectarines), bananas and avocados all continue to ripen after being picked.

7. I have produce ripening all over my house. Sounds silly maybe, but I don't want it crowded on my kitchen countertop. I move it around and turn it over daily.

For a more complete list of produce ripening tips, check out my book, *Kristen's Raw,* available at Amazon.com.

Kristen Suzanne's Tip: Proper Dehydration Techniques

Dehydrating your Raw vegan food at a low temperature is a technique that warms and dries the food while preserving its nutritional integrity. When using a dehydrator, it is recommended that you begin the dehydrating process at a temperature of 130 - 140 degrees for about an hour. Then, lower the temperature to 105 degrees for the remaining time of dehydration. Using a high temperature such as 140 degrees, *in the initial stages of dehydration,* does not destroy the nutritional value of the food. During this initial phase, the food does the most "sweating" (releasing moisture), which cools the food. Therefore, while the temperature of the air circulating *around* the food is about 140 degrees, the food itself is much cooler. These directions apply only when using an Excalibur Dehydrator because of their Horizontal-Airflow Drying System. Furthermore, I am happy to only recommend Excalibur dehydrators because of their first-class products and customer service. For details, visit the *Raw Kitchen Essential Tools* section of my website at KristensRaw.com/store.

MY YIELD AND SERVING AMOUNTS NOTED IN THE RECIPES

Each recipe in this book shows an approximate amount that the recipe yields (the quantity it makes). I find that "one serving" to me might be considered two servings to someone else, or vice versa. Therefore, I tried to use an "average" when listing the serving amount. Don't let that stop you from eating a two-serving dish in one sitting, if it seems like the right amount for you. It simply depends on how hungry you are.

WHAT IS THE DIFFERENCE BETWEEN CHOPPED, DICED, AND MINCED?

Chop

This gives relatively uniform cuts, but doesn't need to be perfectly neat or even. You'll often be asked to chop something before putting it into a blender or food processor, which is why it doesn't have to be uniform size since it'll be getting blended or pureed.

Dice

This produces a nice cube shape, and can be different sizes, depending on which you prefer. This is great for vegetables.

Mince

This produces an even, very fine cut, typically used for fresh herbs, onions, garlic and ginger.

Julienne

This is a fancy term for long, rectangular cuts.

WHAT EQUIPMENT DO I NEED FOR MY NEW RAW FOOD KITCHEN?

I go into much more detail regarding the perfect setup for your Raw vegan kitchen in my book, *Kristen's Raw,* which is a must read for anybody who wants to learn the easy ways to succeed with living the Raw vegan lifestyle. Here are the main pieces of equipment you'll want to get you going:

1. An excellent chef's knife (6 - 8 inches in length – non-serrated). Of everything you do with Raw food, you'll be chopping and cutting the most, so invest in a great knife. This truly makes doing all the chopping really fun!

2. Blender

3. Food Processor (get a 7 or 10-cup or more)

4. Juicer

5. Spiralizer or Turning Slicer

6. Dehydrator – Excalibur® is the best company by far and is available at KristensRaw.com

7. Salad spinner

8. Other knives (paring, serrated)

For links to online retailers that sell my favorite kitchen tools and foods, visit KristensRaw.com/store.

SOAKING AND DEHYDRATING NUTS AND SEEDS

This is an important topic. When using nuts and seeds in Raw vegan foods, you'll find that recipes sometimes call for them to be "soaked" or "soaked and dehydrated." Here is the low-down on the importance and the difference between the two.

Why should you soak your nuts and seeds?

Most nuts and seeds come packed by Mother Nature with enzyme inhibitors, rendering them harder to digest. These inhibitors essentially shut down the nuts' and seeds' metabolic activity, rendering them dormant – for as long as they need to be – until they detect a moisture-rich environment that's suitable for germination (e.g., rain). By soaking your nuts and seeds, you trick the nuts into "waking up," shutting off the inhibitors so that the enzymes can become active. This greatly enhances the nuts' digestibility for you and is highly recommended if you want to experience Raw vegan food in the healthiest way possible.

Even though you'll want to soak the nuts to activate their enzymes, before using them, you'll need to re-dry them and grind them down anywhere from coarse to fine (into a powder almost like flour), depending on the recipe. To dry them, you'll need a dehydrator. (If you don't own a dehydrator yet, then, if a recipe calls for "soaked and dehydrated," just skip the soaking part; you can use the nuts or seeds in the dry form that you bought them).

Drying your nuts (but not yet grinding them) is a great thing to do before storing them in the freezer or refrigerator (preferably in glass mason jars). They will last a long time and you'll always have them on hand, ready to use.

In my recipes, always use nuts and seeds that are "soaked and dehydrated" (that is, *dry*) unless otherwise stated as "soaked" (wet).

Some nuts and seeds don't have to follow the enzyme inhibitor rule; therefore, they don't need to be soaked. These are:

- Macadamia nuts
- Brazil nuts
- Pine nuts
- Hemp seeds
- Most cashews

An additional note... there are times when the recipe will call for soaking, even though it's for a type of nut or seed without enzyme inhibitors, such as Brazil nuts. The logic behind this is to help *soften* the nuts so they blend into a smoother texture, especially if you don't have a high-powered blender. This is helpful when making nut milks, soups and sauces.

Instructions for "Soaking" and "Soaking and Dehydrating" Nuts

"Soaking"

The general rule to follow: Any nuts or seeds that require soaking can be soaked overnight (6 - 10 hours). Put the required amount of nuts or seeds into a bowl and add enough water to cover by about an inch or so. Set them on your counter overnight. The following morning, or 6 - 10 hours after you soaked them, drain and rinse them. They are now ready to eat or use in a recipe. At this point, they need to be refrigerated in an airtight container (preferably a glass mason jar) and they'll have a shelf life of about 3 days maximum. Only soak the amount you're going to need or eat, unless you plan on dehydrating them right away.

A note about flax seeds and chia seeds... these don't need to be soaked if your recipe calls for grinding them into a powder. Some recipes will call to soak the seeds in their "whole-seed" form, before making crackers and bread, because they create a very gelatinous and binding texture when soaked. You can soak flax or chia seeds in a ratio of one-part seeds to two-parts water, and they can be soaked for as short as 1 hour and up to 12 hours. At this point, they are ready to use (don't drain them). Personally, when I use flax seeds, I usually grind them and don't soak them. It's hard for your body to digest "whole" flax seeds, even if they are soaked. It's much easier for your body to assimilate the nutrients when they're ground to a flax meal.

"Soaking and Dehydrating"

Follow the same directions for soaking. Then, after draining and rinsing the nuts, spread them out on a mesh dehydrator sheet and dehydrate them at 140 degrees for one hour. Lower the temperature to 105 degrees and dehydrate them until they're completely dry, which can take up to 24 hours.

Please note, all nuts and seeds called for in my recipes will always be "Raw and Organic" and "Soaked and Dehydrated" unless the recipe calls for soaking.

ALMOND PULP

Some of my recipes call for "almond pulp," which is really easy to make. After making your fresh almond milk (see *Nut Milk* recipe, p. 25) and straining it through a "nut milk bag," (available at NaturalZing.com or you can use a paint strainer bag from the hardware store – much cheaper), you will find a nice, soft pulp inside the bag. Turn the bag inside out and flatten the pulp out onto a paraflex dehydrator sheet with a spatula or your hand. Dehydrate the pulp at 140 degrees for one hour, then lower the temperature to 105 degrees and continue dehydrating until the almond pulp is dry (up to 24 hours). Break the pulp into chunks and store in the freezer until you're ready to use it. Before using the almond pulp, grind it into a flour in your blender or food processor.

SOY LECITHIN

Some recipes (desserts, in particular) will call for soy lecithin, which is extracted from soybean oil. This optional ingredient is not Raw. If you use soy lecithin, I highly recommend using a brand that is "non-GMO," meaning it was processed without any genetically modified ingredients (a great brand is Health Alliance®). Soy lecithin helps your dessert (cheesecake, for example) maintain a firmer texture.

That said, it's certainly not necessary. If an amount isn't suggested, a good rule of thumb is to use 1 teaspoon per 1 cup total recipe volume.

ICE CREAM FLAVORINGS

When making Raw vegan ice cream, it's better to use alcohol-free extracts so they freeze better.

SWEETENERS

The following is a list of sweeteners that you might see used in my recipes. It's important to know that the healthiest sweeteners are fresh whole fruits, including fresh dates. That said, dates sometimes compromise texture in recipes. As a chef, I look for great texture, and as a health food advocate, I lean towards fresh dates. But as a consultant helping people embrace a Raw vegan lifestyle, I'm also supportive of helping them transition, which sometimes means using raw agave nectar, or some other easy-to-use sweetener that might not have the healthiest ranking in the Raw food world, but is still much healthier than most sweeteners used in the Standard American Diet.

Most of my recipes can use pitted dates in place of raw agave nectar. There is some debate among Raw food enthusiasts as to whether agave nectar is Raw. The company I use (Madhava®) claims to be Raw and says they do not heat their Raw agave nectar above 118 degrees. If however, you still want to eat the healthiest of sweeteners, then bypass the raw agave nectar and use pitted dates. In most recipes, you can simply substitute 1 - 2 pitted dates for 1 tablespoon of raw agave nectar. Dates won't give you a super creamy texture, but the texture can be improved by making a "date paste" (pureeing pitted and soaked dates – with their soak water, plus some additional water, if necessary – in a food processor fitted with the "S" blade). This, of course, takes a little extra time.

If using raw agave nectar is easier and faster for you, then go ahead and use it; just be sure to buy the Raw version that says they don't heat the agave above 118 degrees (see KristensRaw.com/store for links to this product). And, again, if you're looking to go as far as you can on the spectrum of health, then I recommend using pitted dates. Most of my recipes say raw agave nectar because that is most convenient for people.

Agave Nectar

There are a variety of agave nectars on the market, but again, not all of them are Raw. Make sure it is labeled "Raw" on the bottle *as well as claiming that it isn't processed above 118 degrees*. Just because the label says "Raw" does not necessarily mean it is so... do a double check and make sure it also claims not to be heated above the 118 degrees cut-off. Agave nectar is noteworthy for having a low glycemic index.

Dates

Dates are probably the healthiest of sweeteners, because they're a fresh whole food. Fresh organic dates are filled with nutrition, including calcium and magnesium. I like to call dates, "Nature's Candy."

Feel free to use dates instead of agave or honey in Raw vegan recipes. If a recipe calls for 1/2 cup of raw agave, then you can substitute with approximately 1/2 cup of pitted dates. You can also make your own date sugar by dehydrating pitted dates and then grinding them down. This is a great alternative to Rapadura®.

Honey

Most honey is technically raw, but it is not vegan by most definitions of "vegan" because it is produced by animals, who therefore are at risk of being mistreated. While honey does not have the health risks associated with animal byproducts such as eggs or dairy, it can spike the body's natural sugar levels. Agave nectar has a lower, healthier glycemic index and can replace any recipe you find that calls for honey, in a 1 to 1 ratio.

Maple Syrup

Maple syrup is made from boiled sap of the maple tree. It is not considered Raw, but some people still use it as a sweetener in certain dishes.

Rapadura®

This is a dried sugarcane juice, and it's not Raw. It is, however, an unrefined and unbleached organic whole-cane sugar. It imparts a nice deep sweetness to your recipes, even if you only use a little. Feel free to omit it if you'd like to adhere to a strictly Raw program. You can substitute Rapadura with home-made date sugar (see Dates above).

Stevia

This is from the leaf of the stevia plant. It has a sweet taste and doesn't elevate blood sugar levels. It's very sweet, so you'll want to use much less stevia than you would any other sweetener. My mom actually grows her own stevia. It's a great addition in fresh smoothies, for example, to add some sweetness without the calories. You can use the white powdered or liquid version from the store, but these are not Raw. When possible, the best way to have stevia is grow it yourself.

Yacon Syrup

This sweetener has a low glycemic index, making it very attractive to some people. It has a molasses-type flavor that is nice and rich. You can replace raw agave with this sweetener in my recipes, but make sure to get the Raw variety, available at NaturalZing.com. They offer a few different yacon syrups, including one in particular that is not heat-treated. Be sure to choose that one.

SUN-DRIED TOMATOES

By far, the best sun-dried tomatoes are those you make yourself with a dehydrator. If you don't have a dehydrator, make sure you buy the "dry" sun-dried tomatoes, usually found in the bulk section of your health food market. Don't buy the kind that are packed in a jar of oil.

Also... don't buy sun-dried tomatoes if they're really dark (almost black) because these just don't taste as good. Again, I recommend making them yourself if you truly want the freshest flavor possible. It's really fun to do!

EATING WITH YOUR EYES

Most of us, if not all, naturally eat with our eyes before taking a bite of food. So, do yourself a favor and make your eating experience the best ever with the help of a simple, gorgeous presentation. Think of it this way, with real estate, it's always *location, location, location*, right? Well, with food, it's always *presentation, presentation, presentation*.

Luckily, Raw food does this on its own with all of its naturally vibrant and bright colors. But I take it even one step farther – I use my best dishes when I eat. I use my beautiful wine glasses for my smoothies and juices. I use my fancy goblets for many of my desserts. Why? Because I'm worth it. And, so are you! Don't save your good china just for company. Believe me, you'll notice the difference. Eating well is an attitude, and when you take care of yourself, your body will respond in kind.

ONLINE RESOURCES FOR GREAT PRODUCTS

For a complete and detailed list of my favorite kitchen tools, products, and various foods (all available online), please visit: KristensRaw.com/store.

BOOK RECOMMENDATIONS

I highly recommend reading the following life-changing books.

- *Diet for a New America*, by John Robbins
- *The Food Revolution*, by John Robbins
- *The China Study*, by T. Colin Campbell
- *Skinny Bitch*, by Rory Freedman

MEASUREMENT CONVERSIONS

1 tablespoon = 3 teaspoons

1 ounce = 2 tablespoons

1/4 cup = 4 tablespoons

1/3 cup = 5 1/3 tablespoons

1 cup

= 8 ounces

= 16 tablespoons

= 1/2 pint

1/2 quart

= 1 pint

= 2 cups

1 gallon

= 4 quarts

= 8 pints

= 16 cups

= 128 ounces

BASIC RECIPES TO KNOW

Nourishing Rejuvelac

Yield 1 gallon

Rejuvelac is a cheesy-tasting liquid that is rich in enzymes and healthy flora to support a healthy intestine and digestion.

Get comfortable making this super easy recipe because its use goes beyond just drinking it between meals.

1 cup soft wheat berries, rye berries, or a mixture

water

Place the wheat berries in a half-gallon jar and fill the jar with water. Screw the lid on the jar and soak the wheat berries overnight(10 - 12 hours) on your counter. The next morning, drain and rinse them. Sprout the wheat berries for 2 days, draining and rinsing 1 - 2 times a day.

Then, fill the jar with purified water and screw on the lid, or cover with cheesecloth secured with a rubber band. Allow to ferment for 24 - 36 hours, or until the desired tartness is achieved. It should have a cheesy, almost tart/lemony flavor and scent.

Strain your rejuvelac into another glass jar and store in the refrigerator for up to 5 - 7 days. For a second batch using the same sprouted wheat berries, fill the same jar of already sprouted berries with water again, and allow to ferment for 24 hours. Strain off the rejuvelac as you did the time before this. You can do this process yet again, noting that each time the rejuvelac gets a little weaker in flavor.

Enjoy 1/4 - 1 cup of *Nourishing Rejuvelac* first thing in the morning and/or between meals. It's best to start with a small amount and work your way up as your body adjusts.

Suggestion:

- For extra nutrition and incredible flavor, *Nourishing Rejuvelac* can be used in various recipes such as Raw vegan cheeses, desserts, smoothies, soups, dressings and more. Simply use it in place of the water required by the recipe.

Crème Fraiche

Yield approximately 2 cups

> 1 cup cashews, soaked 1 hour, drained, and rinsed
>
> 1/4 - 1/2 cup *Nourishing Rejuvelac* (see p. 23)
>
> 1 - 2 tablespoons raw agave nectar

Blend the ingredients until smooth. Store in an airtight glass mason jar for up to 5 days. This freezes well, so feel free to make a double batch for future use.

Nut/Seed Milk (regular)

Yield 4 - 5 cups

The creamiest nut/seed milk traditionally comes from hemp seeds, cashews, pine nuts, Brazil nuts or macadamia nuts, although I'm also a huge fan of milks made from walnuts, pecans, hazelnuts, almonds, sesame seeds, and others.

This recipe does not include a sweetener, but when I'm in the mood for a little sweetness, I add a couple of pitted dates or a squirt of raw agave nectar. Yum!

> 1 1/2 cups nuts, soaked 6 - 12 hours, drained and rinsed
>
> 3 1/4 cups water
>
> pinch Himalayan crystal salt, optional

Blend the ingredients until smooth and deliciously creamy. For an even *extra creamy* texture, strain your nut/seed milk through a nut milk bag.

Sweet Nut/Seed Cream (thick)

Yield 2 - 3 cups

>   1 cup nuts or seeds, soaked 6 - 8 hours, drained and rinsed
>
>   1 - 1 1/2 cups water, more if needed
>
>   2 - 3 tablespoons raw agave nectar or 2 - 3 dates, pitted
>
>   1/2 teaspoon vanilla extract, optional

Blend all of the ingredients until smooth.

Raw Mustard

Yield approximately 1 1/2 - 2 cups

>   1 - 2 tablespoons yellow mustard seeds (depending on how "hot" you want it), soaked 1 - 2 hours
>
>   1 1/2 cups extra virgin olive oil or hemp oil
>
>   1 1/2 tablespoons dry mustard powder
>
>   2 tablespoons apple cider vinegar
>
>   2 tablespoons fresh lemon juice
>
>   3 dates, pitted and soaked 30-minutes, drained
>
>   1/2 cup raw agave nectar
>
>   1 teaspoon Himalayan crystal salt
>
>   pinch turmeric

Blend all of the ingredients together until smooth. It might be very thick, so if you want, add some water or oil to help thin it out. Adding more oil will help reduce the "heat" if it's too spicy for your taste.

26

Variation:

- *Honey Mustard Version:* Add another 1/3 cup raw agave nectar (or more, depending on how sweet you want it)

My Basic Raw Mayonnaise

Yield about 2 1/2 cups

People tell me all the time how much they like this recipe.

1 cup cashews, soaked 1 - 2 hours, drained

1/2 teaspoon paprika

2 cloves garlic

1 teaspoon onion powder

3 tablespoons fresh lemon juice

1/4 cup extra virgin olive oil or hemp oil

2 tablespoons parsley, chopped

2 tablespoons water, if needed

Blend all of the ingredients, except the parsley, until creamy. Pulse in the parsley. *My Basic Raw Mayonnaise* will stay fresh for up to one week in the refrigerator.

CHAPTER 2

DRESSINGS

PHOTOS OF RECIPES AVAILABLE AT:

KristensRaw.com/photos

The following recipes in this book have been photographed. See KristensRaw.com/photos for pretty pictures of:

- Cayenne Tahini Dressing
- Kristen Suzanne's Rockin' Kale Salad (see cover)
- Summer Picnic Slaw
- Grapefruit-Jicama Salad with Creamy Avocado
- My Spicy Vegetable Tango
- Deviled Mango Dressing on Cosmic Carrots

I always like to get feedback on my photographs! (In addition to hearing your stories about my recipes too!) If you visit the site, please let me know your favorites by writing to me at:

Kristen@KristensRaw.com

DRESSINGS BEFORE THE SALADS?

Why start with dressings before salads? After all, dressing goes on top of salads, so you have to make the salad first... right?

I'll share a little secret with you. The secret to good salads is one word: *dressing*. The dressing is the primary source of any salad's flavor. Sure, there's more to a great salad than just its dressing, but there is no such thing as a great salad that doesn't have a great dressing.

What defines a "great" dressing? That's easy – a truly great dressing is one that makes you want to take another bite of the salad. In fact, when you run out of salad and all that's left is the dressing in the bottom of bowl, a truly great dressing will make you want to go get a little more salad just to soak up the last little bit of dressing!

Most of us think of salads as healthy, but not much more. But we're going to change that here and now. Get ready to get EXCITED about SALAD! It all starts with fabulous dressings, so that's where we're going to start.

SWEET CAPRI DRESSING

Yield 3/4 cup

This dressing celebrates the Isle of Capri where they grow tons of lemons. It's dynamite when served over a grapefruit and avocado salad or over a giant bowl of plain romaine lettuce. I'm telling you, romaine never tasted so good!

Lemons are very good for you. They're alkalizing for your body and an excellent source of vitamin C. But, that's not all. These yellow darlings also have folate, calcium, vitamin A, potassium, and flavonoids (known for fighting cancer and heart disease).

30

1/2 cup extra virgin olive oil

3 tablespoons raw agave nectar

2 tablespoons apple cider vinegar

1/4 cup + 2 tablespoons fresh lemon juice

1 teaspoon Himalayan crystal salt

1/4 teaspoon black pepper

Blend all of the ingredients together.

Serving suggestion:

- Peel and section a pink grapefruit and put on top of some fresh spring greens, along with sliced avocado. Put Sweet Capri Dressing on top and toss to mix well

"BASIL IS LOVE" DRESSING

Yield approximately 1 cup

In Italy, basil is a symbol of love. I'm Italian and grew up eating lots of fresh basil. I find the fragrance intoxicating.

1/2 cup extra virgin olive oil

1/3 cup fresh lemon juice

1/2 teaspoon Italian seasoning

1/4 teaspoon Himalayan crystal salt

1/4 cup fresh basil leaves, chopped

Blend all of the ingredients, except the basil, in a blender until smooth and creamy. Add the basil and pulse to chop for a few seconds.

DELICIOUS CITRUS DRESSING

Yield approximately 1 cup

This dressing is fun, refreshing, and packs a nutritional punch. I'm always asked for the recipe when I make it. The citrus serves up a terrific dose of vitamin C, along with plenty of other nutrients.

All citrus fruits are high in flavonoids, which are known to help fight cancer and heart disease.

   1/4 cup extra virgin olive oil

   1/4 cup fresh orange juice

   1/4 cup fresh lime juice

   1/4 cup fresh lemon juice

   1 tablespoon tamari, wheat-free (add more if desired)

   2 cloves garlic

   1/2 tablespoon fresh ginger, peeled and grated

Blend all of the ingredients together well.

GUACAMOLE SALAD DRESSING

Yield 2 cups

I love guacamole so it only made sense to make a dressing out of it. And, avocado is filled with a whopping 9 grams of dietary fiber (sometimes more!), plus plenty of B-vitamins, including folate – making this an excellent choice of fruit for pregnant ladies. ☺

1/4 cup water

1 avocado, pitted and peeled

2 tablespoons fresh lime juice

1 clove garlic

1 cucumber, peeled and chopped

1 stalk celery, chopped

1/4 cup cilantro, chopped

1/2 teaspoon cumin

1/2 teaspoon Himalayan crystal salt

1/2 teaspoon chili seasoning

Blend all of the ingredients in a blender until creamy. Then, sit back and enjoy a salad like never before!

JOLLY GREEN DRESSING

Yield approximately 3/4 cup

Spinach is a terrific source of iron (the vitamin C in the lemon juice below helps your body absorb this more efficiently), fiber, vitamin K, calcium, lutein, vitamin A, manganese, folate (can help improve cognition), magnesium, and glycolipids (phytonutrients known to help fight cancer growth). Okay, so are you convinced that you should have spinach in your diet after reading how awesome it is?

1/4 cup extra virgin olive oil or hemp oil

1 teaspoon apple cider vinegar

2 teaspoons fresh lemon juice

(continued)

1/4 cup spinach, packed

1/2 avocado, pitted and peeled

1 teaspoon raw agave nectar

1/4 - 1/2 teaspoon Himalayan crystal salt

1 sprig fresh dill or 1/8 teaspoon dried dill

1 sprig fresh thyme or 1/8 teaspoon dried thyme

Place all of the ingredients in a blender and blend until smooth. Enjoy!

OPEN SESAME DRESSING

Yield approximately 1 1/2 cups

One of my favorite ways to eat this dressing is to pair it with a plate of chopped baby bok choy. Sesame seeds are among the highest in being able to help lower cholesterol because of their phytosterol content. But, that's not all; they're also full of iron, potassium, manganese, copper, protein, fiber, and more.

1/2 cup ground sesame seeds

3/4 cup water, or more

1 tablespoon green onion, chopped

1 teaspoon fresh ginger, grated

1 teaspoon kelp powder

4 teaspoons tamari, wheat-free

2 tablespoons fresh lemon juice

1 clove garlic

Place the sesame seeds and water in a blender and blend until smooth, adding more water until you reach your desired consistency. Add the remaining ingredients and blend until smooth.

YIN-YANG DRESSING

Yield 2+ cups

Fresh ginger is the "queen" of herbs in my life (the "king" is garlic), and you'll always find fresh ginger in my refrigerator or freezer.

Fresh ginger is a terrific source of powerful antioxidants, which have been noted for helping fight cancer and inflammation. Ginger is also known as a "warming" herb because of its amazing circulatory properties. And, as you probably know, it's reputed for helping ease an upset tummy. (Storage: when wrapped tightly, you can store fresh, unpeeled ginger in your refrigerator for up to 3 weeks and frozen for up to 6 months.)

    1 cup young Thai coconut water
    1 cup young Thai coconut meat
    2/3 cup raw tahini
    3 tablespoons fresh ginger, grated
    2 1/2 tablespoons raw agave nectar
    2 tablespoons tamari, wheat-free
    2 tablespoons fresh lemon juice
    2 tablespoons fresh lime juice
    1/2 teaspoon chili powder
    1/2 teaspoon ground turmeric
    1 clove garlic

Combine all of the ingredients in a blender and puree until smooth, adding water as needed for a beautiful dressing consistency.

KUMQUAT DRESSING

Yield 3 - 4 servings

If you can get organic kumquats, then this dressing is something you have to try. It's deliciously unique and full of brightness.

Kumquats look like miniature oranges with a slightly oval shape. You eat them whole without peeling or anything (very low maintenance). They're tiny, not getting much larger than a cherry tomato or grape tomato. The neat thing about eating kumquats, whole, is that the experience you have when biting into it changes with each bite. You'll get tart first, then it changes to sweet, or vice versa. The inside of a cute little kumquat (and, they are cute! Now I know why my mom called me her "kumquat" when I was a little kid... okay, maybe it wasn't because I was cute, rather that I was sour and tart at times, then super sweet others – ha ha – you'll have to ask her!)... anyway, the inside of a kumquat can be a little dry (this is normal) and they're best stored in the refrigerator, where they can last up to a month.

8 - 10 kumquats, whole

1/4 - 1/2 cup young Thai coconut water (depending on desired consistency)

2 tablespoons raw tahini

1/4 teaspoon Himalayan crystal salt (or more to taste)

Blend all of the ingredients until smooth and creamy.

CAYENNE TAHINI DRESSING

See photo at KristensRaw.com/photos.

Yield 1 cup

I love this dressing because it makes any salad absolutely scrumptious. You can also use it as a decadent sauce drizzled over fresh raw vegetables such as asparagus or freshly sliced cucumbers.

The cayenne adds such a nice kick to it. I've seen people licking their salad bowls after having this (never thought I'd see someone licking a "salad bowl" – but it is delicious!)

1/2 cup raw tahini
1/4 - 1/2 cup water (or extra virgin olive oil)*
3 tablespoons fresh lemon juice & lime juice mixture**
1/4 -1/2 teaspoon cayenne pepper
1/4 - 1/2 teaspoon Himalayan crystal salt

Blend all of the ingredients until smooth.

* Add more water as needed, or use a mixture of water and oil if you're aiming for a really creamy dressing.

** You can use all lemon juice or all lime juice. I like the combination. I prefer a zesty flavor with this dressing, so sometimes I even add more citrus.

Variations:

- Use orange juice instead of lemon and lime juice
- Add a pinch of cinnamon and/or cumin

EASY GARLIC AVOCADO DRESSING

Yield 1 1/2 cups

This great little dressing is a gorgeous light green color and packs a flavorful punch. My family loves the combination of the delicious garlic with the zesty lime juice. And, it's super easy to make... should take you only about three minutes.
Easy + Delicious + Nutritious = Super Awesome!

1/2 cup water
1/4 cup fresh lime juice
1/4 cup fresh orange juice
1 avocado, pitted & peeled
2 cloves garlic
1/2 teaspoon Himalayan crystal salt

Blend all of the ingredients in your blender until smooth and creamy. Enjoy!

DEVILED MANGO DRESSING ON COSMIC CARROTS

See photo at KristensRaw.com/photos.

Yield 2 - 3 servings

This dressing is gorgeous, vibrant and absolutely delicious. I get many compliments on it. And, it's packed with a strong nutritional punch.
The salad portion serves about 2 - 3 as written here, but the dressing will yield about 1 1/2 cups, so you'll have leftover

dressing to use over the next few days for more salads or as a dip for fresh veggies.

The Dressing

1/4 cup water

2 tablespoons olive oil

2 tablespoons coconut oil

1 tablespoon fresh lemon juice

1 tablespoon vegan, organic white wine

1 mango, peeled, pitted, and chopped

2 soft dates, pitted

1 teaspoon garlic powder

1/4 teaspoon Himalayan crystal salt

1/8 teaspoon cayenne pepper

The Salad

4 - 6 carrots, sliced into thin rounds, using a mandoline or V-slicer

4 - 6 leaves fresh basil, chopped

Blend all of the dressing ingredients together until creamy.

Plate the sliced carrots on individual serving plates, drizzle a few tablespoons of the dressing on top of each portion and sprinkle on some fresh chopped basil. Store the leftover dressing to use the next few days.

TOMATO EXTRAVANGANZA

Yield 4 servings

Sometimes the best things in life are the simplest things in life. This recipe and the serving suggestions below make for a wonderfully simple and healthy treat.

Tomatoes are a good source of vitamin C, potassium, and phytonutrients. I keep my tomatoes stored on my counter until I'm ready to eat them. If you store them in your refrigerator, then they can get "mealy", which is an unpopular texture for many people.

1 cup parsley, chopped

2 cups tomatoes, chopped

1/3 cup extra virgin olive oil

1/4 cup fresh lemon juice

1/4 teaspoon pepper

1/4 teaspoon Himalayan crystal salt (or more to taste)

1/4 cup onions, chopped

Blend all of the ingredients, except the onions, until smooth. Pulse in the onions. Serve over chopped vegetables or on top of a wonderful, crisp romaine salad.

Variations:

- Blend in a clove of garlic
- Add 1 - 3 teaspoons of dried herbs and flavorings that you love, one at a time (tasting as you go) or 1 - 2 tablespoons of your favorite fresh herbs

Serving suggestions:

- Place 1 head of cauliflower or broccoli in the food processor, fitted with the "S" blade, and process until coarsely ground or in chunks (your preference). Then, add the dressing, along with 1/2 - 1 teaspoon salt and pulse it in
- Add 2 avocados, pitted, peeled and chopped on top of some hearty romaine lettuce and pour this dressing on top

EASY FRUIT AND OIL DRESSING

Yield approximately 1/2 cup

This dressing is very simple and has its place in your library of recipes. Use it as a simple recipe that's really fast to make or use it as a base on which to build by adding other layers of flavor. Don't forget to write down anything you add to it!

    1/4 cup extra virgin olive oil
    1/2 cup fresh orange juice or fresh pineapple juice
    1 mango, peeled, pitted and chopped
    1/8 teaspoon Himalayan crystal salt, optional

Blend all of the ingredients and serve on your favorite garden fresh salads.

BELLA'S PEPPER DRESSING

Yield 4 servings

I wanted to make something in honor of my mom's spunky little Maltese dog, Bella. This dressing matches her name *and* personality perfectly with the peppers in it, which bring different personalities to the dressing.

1 red bell pepper, destemmed, seeded and chopped

1 yellow bell pepper, destemmed, seeded and chopped

1 - 2 jalapeno or Serrano peppers, destemmed and seeded

1/4 cup fresh lemon juice

1/3 cup extra virgin olive oil

1/2 - 1 teaspoon Himalayan crystal salt

1/2 cup cilantro, chopped

1/2 cup parsley, chopped

Black pepper, to taste

Blend all of the peppers, lemon juice, extra virgin olive oil, and salt until creamy. Pulse in the cilantro and parsley. Season with black pepper, to taste.

Variation:

- Replace the 1/2 cup cilantro with 1/3 cup fresh basil

MONSOON MAYONNAISE

Yield approximately 1 cup

Brazil nuts are loaded with selenium, which have been shown to have a protective effect against cancer. They also contain calcium, protein, and fiber. Ever since I was a little girl, I have LOVED snacking on Brazil nuts. Yum!!!

42

1 cup Brazil nuts, soaked 1 hour, drained & rinsed

2 tablespoons water, or more for desired consistency

1 tablespoon raw agave nectar

1 tablespoon apple cider vinegar

1 tablespoon fresh lemon juice

1/2 teaspoon mustard powder

1/2 teaspoon Himalayan crystal salt

1/3 - 1/2 cup extra virgin olive oil (depending on thickness desired)

pinch black pepper

Blend all of the ingredients together until creamy. Use this delicious mayonnaise on fresh salad wraps, as a dip for vegetable crudités, or as a hearty dressing on top of a crisp romaine salad.

COWGIRL MARINADE AND DRESSING

Yield 3/4 cup

I like to play in the kitchen when I'm preparing food, infusing lots of playful energy and love into the food. So, when I make this recipe, I wear one of my many cowgirl hats and shout out a few "Yee Haws!" (this always makes my husband laugh).

1/2 cup extra virgin olive oil

3 tablespoons fresh lime juice

2 tablespoons water

1 - 2 tablespoons organic, vegan white wine, optional

(continued)

1 tablespoon scallions, minced (white and green parts)

1 - 2 cloves garlic

1/2 teaspoon cumin

1 teaspoon raw agave nectar

1/4 teaspoon Himalayan crystal salt (or more to taste)

1/4 teaspoon black pepper

Blend all of the ingredients together in a blender.

LIGHT-N-LIVELY TAHINI PARSLEY DRESSING

Yield approximately 1 3/4 cup

This is one of those recipes that will be a staple in your household; trust me. It's fragrant, fresh, lively and vibrant. Add to that the fact that it's simple to make, and can be used as a nice light dressing on any salad or poured onto a hearty vegetable dish.

Lemons are wonderful for your health. They are an excellent source of vitamin C. But, that's not all. These yellow darlings also have folate, calcium, vitamin A, potassium, and flavonoids (known for fighting cancer and heart disease).

1/2 cup water

1/2 cup fresh lemon juice

2 tablespoons raw tahini

1 teaspoon cumin

1 clove garlic

(continued)

1/4 - 1/2 teaspoon Himalayan crystal salt, or more to taste

1 cup parsley, chopped

black pepper, to taste

Blend all of the ingredients, except the parsley and black pepper, until smooth. Pulse in the parsley. Season with black pepper, to taste.

Variation:

- Add 4 kalamata olives, pitted and chopped, before blending

ESSENCE DE L'ORANGE DATE SAUCE

Yield approximately 1 cup

This is a beautiful and exquisitely flavored sauce that is sure to please your taste buds.

Dates are like "nature's candy" because they're so sweet. I love dates – big time! Dates have calcium, magnesium, potassium, fiber, and vitamin A.

1/2 cup soft dates, pitted & packed

1 tablespoon fresh lemon juice

1 - 2 tablespoons orange blossom water, or more depending on preference*

1/2 cup water, or more as needed

In a food processor, fitted with the "S" blade, puree the dates with the lemon juice and orange blossom water, adding enough water to make a creamy paste.

* You can find orange blossom water in most Middle Eastern markets, online, and some Whole Food Markets.

Serving suggestion:

- Enjoy this sauce on fresh fruit or vegetables

Variation:

- Add various seasonings such as cinnamon, allspice, cumin, fresh mint, etc. Start with a pinch and taste as you go, adding more if desired. For fresh herbs, start with 1 tablespoon and taste as you go

CINNAMON THYME DRESSING

Yield approximately 1 cup

The thyme offers a wonderful pungent flavor that is slightly mint-like and supports the cinnamon beautifully.

Cinnamon has always been one of my mom's favorite spices so she has been adding it to her recipes most of my life. So much so that my brother and I started teasing her about it when we were growing up.

Well, well, well... what do we have here but a recipe that "I" made which features cinnamon – haha. It turns out that mom knows best (sorry, Mom, it took me twenty-some years to come to this realization!).

Cinnamon rocks the house! It's been said that the compounds in cinnamon can help moderate blood sugar, improve capillary function, fight candida and inflammation, improve digestion, and may help reduce blood pressure.

1 cup extra virgin olive oil

2 tablespoons apple cider vinegar

1/2 teaspoon powdered ginger

1/2 teaspoon cinnamon

1/2 teaspoon paprika

1/2 teaspoon dried thyme leaves

1/2 teaspoon Himalayan crystal salt

1/4 teaspoon black pepper

Blend all of the ingredients together, and enjoy as a delightfully seasoned sauce over your favorite chopped vegetables or served on a nice bed of romaine lettuce. The dressing has a delicious intensity about it with all of the unique flavors, so make sure you use a lettuce that is hearty and can go head-to-head with the dressing.

VITALITY LIME SHALLOT DRESSING

Yield approximately 3/4 cup

This is a deliciously sassy dressing. Limes are filled with phytochemicals known to help prevent oxidative damage to cells.

1/2 cup extra virgin olive oil

1/4 cup fresh lime juice

1 tablespoon shallot, minced

1/2 teaspoon Himalayan crystal salt

1 clove garlic

pinch cayenne pepper

1 tablespoon fresh mint, chopped

Blend all of the ingredients together, except the fresh mint. Pulse in the fresh mint. Enjoy!

LATIN AMERICAN FIESTA VINAIGRETTE

Yield 1 1/4 cups

Talk about party time! This is one of the best salad dressings to bring to a party. It's so delicious. I love making a double batch and using it on my salads all week.

2 tablespoons fresh lime juice

2 tablespoons water

1 tablespoon apple cider vinegar

1 tablespoon chili powder

1 teaspoon raw agave nectar

1/2 teaspoon powdered mustard

1/2 teaspoon garlic, pressed

1/2 teaspoon cumin

1/2 teaspoon Himalayan crystal salt

1/2 teaspoon black pepper

1/8 teaspoon cayenne pepper

1 cup extra virgin olive oil

Blend all of the ingredients together in a blender.

Variation:

- Add fresh herbs: 1/4 cup fresh cilantro or 1/4 cup fresh basil or 2 tablespoons of freshly chopped green onions. *If adding the fresh herbs, add them after you make the dressing base and then pulse them in the blender as the last step*

PEPPERY LEMON-LIME VINAIGRETTE

Yield 1 1/2 cups

This is an extremely popular recipe. I know... it's so simple. It can be used as a flavorfully intense dressing or as a wonderful marinade for mushrooms, green beans, asparagus, etc. I like to marinate sliced zucchini in this and then dehydrate them for some awesome kickin' veggie chips.

- 1 cup extra virgin olive oil
- 1/4 cup + 2 tablespoons fresh lemon juice
- 2 tablespoons fresh lime juice
- 2 cloves garlic
- 3/4 teaspoon Himalayan crystal salt
- 1 teaspoon freshly ground black pepper

Blend all of the ingredients together in a blender.

Variation:

- Swap out the garlic for 1 teaspoon of freshly grated ginger

SECRET GARDEN HERB DRESSING

Yield 1 cup

The fresh herbs in this dressing give it such a delectable flavor.

Olive oil has antioxidants, anti-inflammatory agents, and is known to fight a number of diseases including heart disease, cancer, and dementia.

1/2 cup extra virgin olive oil

3 tablespoons fresh lemon juice

1 1/2 teaspoons raw agave nectar

1 teaspoon freshly grated lemon zest

1/2 teaspoon Himalayan crystal salt

pinch black pepper

2 tablespoons fresh chives, chopped

2 tablespoons fresh parsley, chopped

2 tablespoons fresh dill, chopped

Blend all of the ingredients together, except the chives, parsley, and dill. Then, pulse in the chives, parsley, and dill. Enjoy on your favorite salad or vegetables.

JAMAICAN ME HOT AND CRAZY DRESSING

Yield 2 1/2 cups

Caution: Make this at your own risk. It's extremely hot and spicy and reserved only for the brave. You just might think you're having hot flashes when you eat this. But, it's well worth it! This is one of my absolute favorite dressing recipes. ☺

1 cup extra virgin olive oil

1/4 cup + 2 tablespoons fresh orange juice

2 tablespoons fresh lime juice

2 tablespoons fresh lemon juice

2 tablespoons tamari, wheat-free

1 tablespoon ground allspice

1 tablespoon fresh basil, minced

1 tablespoon raw agave nectar

1/2 teaspoon Himalayan crystal salt

2 teaspoons dried thyme

1 teaspoon black pepper

1 teaspoon ground cinnamon

1/2 teaspoon ground ginger

1/2 - 3/4 teaspoon cayenne pepper

1 teaspoon vanilla extract

1 - 2 habanero peppers, destemmed, seeded and finely minced*

** **IMPORTANT** – When handling hot peppers, put some olive oil on your hands to protect them or wear rubber gloves if you're highly sensitive. Immediately wash your hands, utensils, and counter top after you're done with the hot pepper. BE SURE NOT TO TOUCH YOUR FACE!*

Blend all of the ingredients together in a blender and enjoy on your next salad.

Serving suggestion:

- Use this as a dressing over vegetables, sweet fruit, chopped young Thai coconut, or a hearty salad made with romaine lettuce and/or shredded cabbage

TARRAGON LIME AFFAIR

Yield 1/2 cup

The word "tarragon" originally comes from the French word estragon or "little dragon." I adore its licorice-like flavor. And, I love this dressing because it's so easy to make.

1/2 cup olive oil

1/4 cup fresh lime juice

1/4 - 1/2 teaspoon Himalayan crystal salt

1/8 teaspoon black pepper

3 tablespoons fresh tarragon, chopped or 1 tablespoon dried

Blend all of the ingredients, except the tarragon, until smooth. Pulse in the tarragon.

CHERRY CREAM DRESSING

Yield 4 servings

Cherries are full of some seriously powerful nutrition. This gorgeous dark red fruit is loaded with all kinds of fun "anti" compounds... anti-inflammatory, anti-aging, and anti-cancer.

1 cup cherries, destemmed and pitted

1 avocado, peeled, pitted and chopped

2 tablespoons fresh lime or lemon juice

2 pinches Himalayan crystal salt

Blend all of the delicious ingredients together and enjoy on top of a beautiful salad.

STRAWBERRY GINGER DRESSING (fat-free)

Yield 1 cup

Here is a deliciously fresh dressing to make as a staple in your household (especially during the summer). It's light, fat-free (yay, put extra on!), and is going to add a little pep in your step with the sassy ginger kick in it. It pairs wonderfully with a spinach-based salad (spring mix greens are a touch too bitter and romaine lettuce is a little too heavy, which detracts from the lovely lightness of it).

1 1/2 cups fresh strawberries, destemmed and diced
Juice from 1 orange
1 tablespoon fresh ginger, peeled and grated
2 teaspoons raw agave nectar
1 teaspoon apple cider vinegar
1/4 teaspoon Himalayan crystal salt (or more to taste)

Blend all of the ingredients together until smooth. Enjoy!

ZESTY ITALIAN AVOCADO DRESSING

Yield 1 1/2 cups

This is another one of my favorite recipes (big time!), and I'm sure it'll become one of yours, too. I recommend making two batches, because it's so delicious!

3/4 cup water

Juice of 1 lemon

Juice of 1 lime

1 avocado, pitted and peeled

1 soft date, pitted

1 large clove garlic (or 2 small-medium size cloves)

1 tablespoon Italian seasoning

1/2 teaspoon mustard powder

1/2 teaspoon Himalayan crystal salt (or more to taste)

1/8 teaspoon cayenne pepper

Blend all of the ingredients together until creamy.

CREAMY TAHINI DRESSING

Yield 2 1/2 cups

This dressing is so easy and full of flavor that it'll quickly become a favorite in your household. And, it's loaded with nutrition.

1 cup water

1 cup raw tahini

5 tablespoons fresh lemon juice

1 stalk celery, chopped

1/2 cup carrot, chopped

2 cloves garlic

1/2 teaspoon Himalayan crystal salt (or more to taste)

1/2 teaspoon cayenne pepper

Blend all of the ingredients together until creamy.

GOING GUACAMOLE DRESSING

Yield 2 cups

    Guacamole is one of my favorite foods, so I had to make another dressing recipe based on guacamole principles. It's fabulous!

    Avocadoes are filled with a whopping 9 grams of dietary fiber (sometimes more!), plus plenty of B-vitamins, including folate – making this an excellent choice of fruit for pregnant ladies. ☺

> 1/2 cup water
>
> 1/4 cup fresh lemon or lime juice
>
> 2 avocados, pitted and peeled
>
> 2 cloves garlic
>
> 2 stalks celery, chopped
>
> 1 teaspoon cumin
>
> 1/4 teaspoon coriander
>
> 1/2 teaspoon Himalayan crystal salt (or more to taste)
>
> 1/2 - 1 teaspoon red jalapeno pepper, minced
>
> large handful parsley leaves

    Blend all of the ingredients together, except the parsley, until creamy. Add the parsley and pulse your blender to incorporate it.

CREAMY KICKIN' DRESSING

Yield 2 cups

Prunes are not just for shuffleboard players. They have fiber, iron, vitamins A & C, and potassium.

Get ready for an easy, fun, creamy, and unique dressing that I'm sure you'll be making many times. I receive many emails from customers telling me how much they love this dressing.

1 cup water

1 large avocado, pitted and peeled

2 prunes

juice of 1 lemon

1 tablespoon Mexican seasoning

1/2 teaspoon Himalayan crystal salt (or more to taste)

1/8 teaspoon cayenne pepper

Blend all of the ingredients until creamy.

CHAPTER 3

SALADS

With all of my discussion above about the importance of the dressing, it's important not to ignore all the other features that go into a truly great salad. Many of my dressings taste so good, I'm occasionally tempted to drink them straight out of the jar! But of course, that would be weird, and even I don't do that. (Well, not usually. ☺) I like to think of salads as a way to administer a "just right" amount of dressing in every bite.

If the dressing is for flavor, then everything else in the salad is for texture, nutrition, appearance (especially color), and a contribution to the flavor as well.

THE PERFECT SALAD

I'm often asked for ways to easily incorporate more high-energy Raw foods into life. One of the best methods is with what I call *The Perfect Salad* – a simple way to get tons of high-energy nutrition and health into your life. It starts with a fabulous dressing that is easy to make and a big bowl of chopped vegetables, plus any other goodies you add right before eating. The beauty of this salad is that you can make it twice a week (different variations keep it exciting) and have high-energy, full-of-health-goodness for multiple lunches and dinners.

1. Get a large glass bowl with an airtight lid for the chopped vegetables (mine is 4 quarts).

2. Store the dressing separately in a glass mason jar. (See Chapter 2 for recipes.)

3. Keep the chopped veggies basic with just a few varieties (different colors are appealing to the eye) so that you can make it different the next time thereby increasing variety and fun.

4. Pick a couple days a week where you'll spend about 45 minutes in the kitchen chopping vegetables and making your salad dressing. That's it! When you're ready to eat, it takes you less than three minutes to simply scoop out some vegetables, drizzle your fabulous dressing on top, add any little extras you want (raisins, chopped nuts, olives, or fresh herbs) and voila! You are in high-energy, delicious-nutritious-heaven.

A typical salad for me could include chopped red bell peppers, cucumbers, golden beets, and carrots. The next batch might be green zucchini, celery, yellow bell peppers, and red beets. Another example is shredded purple cabbage, shelled peas, cherry tomatoes, and fennel. And, then, sometimes it's simply chopped cucumbers and carrots. As you can see, the combinations are endless! Note: store chopped beets in a separate container and add to your salad just before serving to prevent the color from bleeding onto your other vegetables.

Occasionally, I also add lettuce just before serving (red or green leaf, romaine, baby spring mix or spinach), but more often than not, I don't. I prefer my salads to be hearty with chunks of fiber filling vegetables and non-sweet fruits so they fill me up and keep me satiated for hours.

CARROT CELERY CELEBRATION

Yield 2 servings

One of the best aspects about this salad is that it's pretty easy on the wallet. Another reason is that it's super easy to prepare. And, yet another reason that this salad is great is because it's full of nutrition.

3 stalks of celery, chopped

2 carrots, grated

3 soft dates, pitted and chopped

2 tablespoons golden raisins

1 tablespoon red onion, minced

3 tablespoons lemon juice

1/4 cup extra virgin olive oil

1/8 teaspoon Himalayan crystal salt (or more to taste)

Combine the celery, carrots, dates, raisins, and onions in a bowl. Add the lemon juice, olive oil, and salt. Toss to mix and celebrate how easy and delicious Raw is!

"GO-BIG OR GO-HOME" FRESH HERB SALAD

Yield 2 servings

This salad is packed with so much nutrition and flavor. I like to serve it as a "mini" salad. Big Flavor, Huge Nutrition, Small Portion.

1/2 cup fresh parsley, chopped

1/2 cup fresh basil, chopped

3 tablespoons fresh oregano leaves, chopped

1 tablespoon fresh marjoram, chopped

3 tablespoons fresh thyme, chopped

2 green scallions, chopped

1/2 cup tomato, diced

3 tablespoons fresh lemon juice

3 - 4 tablespoons extra virgin olive oil or hemp oil

Toss all of the ingredients in a bowl and serve in nice little glass cups. When I serve it, I use little tea cups and saucers, with a crunchy flax cracker on the saucer.

ARTFUL GOURMET SALAD

Everyone will want seconds and thirds of this salad because the chewy, crunchy, savory and sweet will have you begging for more.

You'll need the following *for each serving* of salad:

2 cups spring mix lettuce

1 tablespoon dried cranberries

1 tablespoon raw nuts/seeds, chopped* (preferably sweetened, sprouted, organic, and dehydrated)

1 tablespoon *Fun Leeks* (see recipe, below)

2 - 3 tablespoons *Olive Vinaigrette* Dressing (see recipe, below)

* I usually use my recipe for *Sweet Vanilla Rain Sunflower Seeds*, available in my book, *Kristen Suzanne's EASY Raw*

Vegan Sides & Snacks, but any sweetened, sprouted, organic, and dehydrated nuts or seeds will be wonderful.

FUN LEEKS

2 - 4 leeks*
2 - 3 tablespoons olive oil
1 - 1 1/2 tablespoons tamari, wheat-free
1 - 1 1/2 teaspoons raw agave nectar
juice of 1 - 2 limes

Slice the leeks thinly, rinse well and place in a bowl of water to soak for about 30 - 45 minutes. Drain and rinse well. Place the leeks in a shallow bowl with the olive oil, tamari, agave, and lime juice. Let these marinate for about 15 minutes.

Transfer them to a dehydrator tray (shaking off any excess oil over the bowl beforehand) and dehydrate at a temperature of 140 degrees for 60 minutes. Lower the temperature to 105 degrees and continue dehydrating until somewhat crispy, approximately 10 - 15 hours.

* Dirt likes to hide in leeks, so make sure you wash well.

OLIVE VINAIGRETTE DRESSING

Yield 1 1/4 cups

This is one of my family's favorite dressings. They're always asking me to make it.

1/2 cup water

1/2 cup olive oil

2 tablespoons apple cider vinegar

1 tablespoon fresh lemon juice

2 teaspoons raw agave nectar

1 clove garlic

1/4 teaspoon Himalayan crystal salt

1/2 teaspoon dried oregano

1/4 cup fresh basil

1/2 cup pitted kalamata olives (or any olives of your choice)

Blend all of the ingredients for the dressing except for the basil and olives. Add the basil and olives, and pulse your blender to break them up, but not to blend them completely. This gives the dressing a lovely texture and color. Put your salads together with all of the ingredients listed and enjoy!

BLACK AND WHITE SALAD

Yield 2 - 3 servings

I made this one night when I didn't have much in my refrigerator. It was so delicious I had to write it down and share it with everybody. One of my favorite aspects is the crunch you get from the jicama. It's so refreshing. Try it!

1 medium jicama, peeled and diced

3/4 cup *Black Hummus* (see recipe, below)

1/4 cup raisins

Toss everything in a bowl and eat.

BLACK HUMMUS

Yield approximately 2 cups

I love hummus. This version has a particularly special place in my heart because it's a fun and unique color.

2 zucchini, peeled and chopped
1/2 cup fresh lemon juice
2 cloves garlic
1 1/2 teaspoons cumin
1 teaspoon Himalayan crystal salt
1/4 teaspoon coriander
3/4 cup black tahini*

Blend all of the ingredients in your blender until creamy.

* Online retailer Living Tree Community has black tahini. You can find a link to their website by visiting my Web site at KristensRaw.com/store. You can also find it at some Whole Foods stores.

EARTHLY SALAD

Yield 2 servings

Mushrooms deliver plenty of B-complex vitamins along with essential minerals such as selenium, potassium and copper. Gotta love Mother Nature, she provides well. ☺

2 cups cremini mushrooms, sliced

1/4 cup sweet onions, thinly sliced

1/2 cup parsley, chopped

1/4 cup fresh lemon juice

1/4 cup extra virgin olive oil (or more)

1 teaspoon dried thyme

1/2 teaspoon dried tarragon

1/2 teaspoon dried oregano

1/8 teaspoon Himalayan crystal salt (or more to taste)

Toss all of the ingredients together in a bowl and serve.

SALSA FRESCA

Yield 2 servings

I love eating fresh organic salsa just as I would a regular salad. It's so delicious, juicy, refreshing, and healthy! Enjoy a nice big bowl of it and see for yourself.

4 medium tomatoes (2 seeded), and all diced

2 green onions, thinly sliced

2 tablespoons fresh cilantro, chopped

1 tablespoon fresh lime juice

1 - 2 cloves garlic, pressed

1/4 teaspoon Himalayan crystal salt

pinch cayenne pepper

Combine all of the ingredients in a bowl and enjoy.

Variation:

- Add 2 tablespoons of raw pumpkin seeds or hemp seeds

EASY RAW CARROT AND ONION SALAD

Yield 2 servings

Here is a terrific salad that is easy on the wallet, easy to make, and delicious. It's a terrific complement to any dinner you make, whether it's a Raw dinner or a cooked dinner.

2 large carrots, grated
2 - 3 tablespoons white onion, diced
1/4 cup extra virgin olive oil or hemp oil
1/4 cup golden raisins (or regular raisins)
1/2 teaspoon freshly grated lemon zest
2 tablespoons fresh lemon juice
1/4 teaspoon Himalayan crystal salt (or more to taste)
black pepper, to taste

In a bowl, toss together all of the ingredients. Enjoy this easy to make scrumptious salad.

BUTTERFLY RADISH SALAD

Yield 3 - 4 servings

I love the presentation and feel of this salad because of the delicate rounds that are thinly sliced.

Radishes have fiber, vitamin C, calcium, copper, B-vitamins, potassium, and more.

2 cups radishes, thinly sliced

2 cucumbers, thinly sliced

1/4 cup raisins

1/4 cup kalamata olive, pitted and chopped

1/4 cup extra virgin olive oil or hemp oil

3 tablespoons fresh lemon or lime juice

1/8 - 1/4 teaspoon Himalayan crystal salt (or more to taste)

Place all of the ingredients in a bowl and gently toss.

Variations:

- Add 1 clove of garlic, pressed
- Add 1 tablespoon fresh basil, chopped or 1 teaspoon dried
- Add 1 teaspoon dried chervil

TABOUL-"LIVE"

Yield 2 - 3 servings

This is hands down one of my all-time favorite recipes. When I make it, I eat bowl after bowl after bowl of it. Seriously!

Taboul-"live" has so much amazing nutrition in it. Just look at all of those true super star ingredients... parsley, cilantro, green onions, carrot, bell pepper, avocado, and more. Yowza!!!

1 bunch fresh parsley, chopped

1 bunch fresh cilantro, chopped

1/2 bunch green onions, chopped

2 carrots, diced

1 large yellow bell pepper, destemmed, seeded and diced

2 tomatoes, diced

1 avocado, pitted, peeled, and diced

1/3 cup pine nuts or hemp seeds

3 tablespoons raisins

2 tablespoons olive oil or hemp oil

2 tablespoons fresh lime juice

2 teaspoons raw agave nectar

1/2 teaspoon Himalayan crystal salt

black pepper to taste

Place the parsley, cilantro and green onion in a food processor, fitted with the "S" blade, and pulse until chopped into pieces. Transfer to a large bowl. Add the carrots, yellow bell pepper, tomatoes, avocado, pine nuts (or hemp seeds) and raisins to the parsley mixture. Then, in a small bowl, whisk together the olive oil, lime juice, agave nectar, salt and pepper. Pour this over the salad, gently toss, and enjoy.

Variation:

- Use 1/2 cup diced pineapple and omit the raisins (this is so yummy!)

CELERY PICNIC SALAD

Yield 4 - 5 servings

This is a brilliant salad whether you're going on a picnic or not. In fact, the dressing is so terrific that you'll want to use it for other salads as well!

I love celery. It's one of the top foods used to help treat blood pressure. Celery also contains silicon, which is wonderful for bone health. And, I'm a huge fan of consuming celery as juice in my fresh Plant Blood.

The Salad

1 bunch of celery, chopped (include the leaves for more flavor and nutrition)

1 orange bell pepper, destemmed, seeded and diced

2 scallions, chopped

1 cup corn (cut fresh from the cob) or frozen and thawed

1/2 cup English peas, shelled, or frozen peas thawed*

3/4 cup carrot, diced

1/2 cup sprouted sunflower seeds, optional

1 teaspoon fresh thyme, minced

1 tablespoon fresh basil, chopped

The Dressing

1/2 cup extra virgin olive oil

2 tablespoons *Raw Mustard* (see recipe, p. 26) or regular mustard**

2 tablespoons raw agave nectar

2 tablespoons fresh lime juice

(continued)

2 teaspoons apple cider vinegar

2 tablespoons water

1/4 teaspoon Himalayan crystal salt (or more to taste)

black pepper, to taste

Place all of the ingredients for the salad in a large bowl and toss. For the dressing, blend all of the ingredients together and pour on top of the salad. Toss to coat. Enjoy!

* Not all stores carry English Shelling Peas, so you can omit them or substitute with frozen peas, thawed.

** You can use regular store bought mustard, if you don't have *Raw Mustard.*

KRISTEN SUZANNE'S ROCKIN' KALE SALAD

See photo on cover and at KristensRaw.com/photos.

Yield 2 - 3 servings

The colors in this salad are so vibrant and appealing to the eye. It's truly a bowl of health and you'll be coming back for more. I promise.

Kale is a super food in my book. Its nutrient profile makes it one of the healthiest foods to eat (or drink in fresh Plant Blood!). It has protein, vitamins A, C & K, calcium, folate, iron, and some major butt-kicking phytonutrients for helping fight cancer. I make sure to have kale in some form in my diet on a weekly basis, either in a salad, green smoothie, or Plant Blood.

1 large bunch curly kale, destemmed and torn into bite size pieces*

1 large avocado, pitted, peeled and chopped

1 medium tomato, chopped

1 cucumber, diced

1 orange or yellow bell pepper, destemmed, seeded and chopped

1 - 2 cloves garlic, pressed

2 1/2 tablespoons fresh lemon juice

3 soft dates, pitted and chopped

1/2 teaspoon Himalayan crystal salt

pinch black pepper

pinch nutmeg

2 tablespoons dried cranberries or raisins

2 tablespoons hemp seeds

Place the kale in a large bowl. Add the rest of the ingredients, except for the hemp seeds.

Use your hands and massage all of the ingredients well (yes, go ahead and squish the avocado, tomatoes, and cucumbers with your hands!) This really incorporates the avocado and fresh juices from the tomatoes, cucumbers, and lemon juice, with the kale, salt, pepper and nutmeg. Messy? Nah. It's fun ☺

Sprinkle on the hemp seeds. Give a quick toss and enjoy.

* When using curly kale, make sure you wash it well so you get out any hidden dirt.

Variations (try one, or all, of the following):

- Use Swiss chard instead of kale

- Use chopped macadamia nuts, pistachio nuts, or pine nuts in place of the hemp seeds
- Add 1 - 2 tablespoons fresh basil, chopped
- Add 1/2 cup fresh corn from the cob (delicious!)
- Add 2 tablespoons chopped green and/or kalamata olives (Mega yum!)
- Add 1/2 cup chopped, fresh pineapple

ASIAN SESAME CUCUMBERS

Yield 1 - 2 servings

I love cucumbers. They're refreshing, cooling, and wonderful for your skin. This is a delicious little salad to serve alongside your next dinner.

3 tablespoons flax oil or extra virgin olive oil

2 tablespoons fresh lemon juice

1 tablespoon fresh chives, chopped

2 teaspoons tamari, wheat-free

black pepper, to taste

1 large cucumber, thinly sliced

1 tablespoon raw sesame seeds, hulled

Whisk together the oil, lemon juice, chives, tamari and pepper. Combine the dressing in a bowl with the cucumber and sprinkle with the sesame seeds.

Variation:

- Replace the cucumbers with 2 - 3 stalks of bok choy, thinly chopped

FANCY ARUGULA SALAD

Yield 2 servings

This dressing is fabulous and can be used on any salad. Arugula is loaded with antioxidants and minerals (which help aid with detoxification and fight cancer), is super low in calories, and has a lovely peppery type flavor.

The Salad

1/2 bunch arugula
1/4 cup walnuts, chopped

The Dressing

2 tablespoons organic, vegan white wine
1 tablespoon fresh lemon juice
1/2 teaspoon *Raw Mustard** (see recipe, p. 26)
1/2 teaspoon raw agave nectar
pinch Himalayan crystal salt
pinch black pepper
3 tablespoons extra virgin olive oil

Whisk all of the dressing ingredients together. Place the arugula on two plates topped with the chopped walnuts. Pour the dressing over the salads and serve.

* If you don't have *Raw Mustard* already made, then don't let that stop you from making this awesome salad. Although not

Raw, you can substitute with store bought mustard from a bottle.

ITALIAN BREAD SALAD

Yield 3 - 4 servings

This salad reminds me of Sundays when I was growing up. In our Italian family, we always had Italian Bread Salad and I couldn't wait to gobble it up. Here is my healthier version... that I continue to enjoy on Sundays. I just love tradition sometimes.

The Salad

1 1/2 cups cherry tomatoes, cut in half

1 cup cucumber, seeded and chopped

1/4 cup red onion, diced

3 tablespoons fresh basil, minced

3 tablespoons fresh parsley, chopped

2/3 cup pumpkin seeds

1 head romaine lettuce, chopped or torn into bite size pieces

The Dressing

1/4 cup extra virgin olive oil

1/4 cup flaxseed oil

Juice of one lemon

(continued)

73

1 tablespoon apple cider vinegar

1 teaspoon raw agave nectar

1/2 teaspoon dried oregano

1/2 teaspoon Himalayan crystal salt (or more to taste)

1/2 teaspoon black pepper

Blend all of the dressing ingredients together. Pour over the salad mixture and toss well to coat.

Variations:

- Blend in a clove of organic garlic to the dressing for more nutrition (and flavor)
- Add 2 tablespoons of dried currants or raisins

JICAMA SOUL SLAW (fat-free)

Yield 3 - 4 servings

This is a great slaw for people watching their calorie intake because it's fat free. It's crunchy and refreshing, two of the things I love about jicama.

The Salad

4 cups jicama, peeled and shredded

3/4 cup golden raisins

The Dressing

1 teaspoon fresh lemon zest
1 teaspoon fresh lime zest
1/4 cup fresh lime juice
1 teaspoon Himalayan crystal salt
1/4 teaspoon white pepper

Shred the jicama using a food processor, fitted with the shredding plate. Transfer to a bowl and add the raisins. Whisk together the ingredients for the dressing and pour over the jicama. Gently toss. Let the salad sit for ten minutes before serving.

Serving suggestion:

- If you're going to a party, then keep the jicama in a separate container from the dressing and combine them at the party ten minutes before serving

BOK CHOY POWER SALAD WITH BLACK ORIENT DRESSING

Yield 3 - 4 servings

This is a deliciously fun salad because the dressing is black. I call it a "power salad" because it will fill your body with powerful nutrients (just look at all of those top-notch ingredients!). For example, bok choy contains indoles, which are shown to lower the risk for cancer. But that's not all. Bok choy is also filled with potassium, calcium, vitamin A, and beta-carotene. Plus, it's ultra low in calories. ☺

The salad portion serves about four, but the dressing yield will be about 1 3/4 cups (so you'll have left over dressing to use over the next few days for more salads or as a dip for fresh veggies).

The Salad

2 heads bok choy, chopped

2 cucumbers, chopped

2 tomatoes, chopped

2 carrots, chopped

The Dressing

3/4 cup water

1/2 cup zucchini, peeled and chopped

1/2 cup raw black tahini

2 tablespoons tamari, wheat-free

1 3/4 tablespoons fresh lemon juice

1 tablespoon hemp seeds

1 tablespoon raw agave nectar

1 clove garlic

2 teaspoons fresh ginger, peeled and grated

1/8 teaspoon cinnamon

dash cayenne pepper

Blend all of the dressing ingredients in a blender until smooth. Serve some of the dressing over the bok choy salad.

"TENNESSEE VOLUNTEERS" SLAW

Yield 3 - 4 servings

I love sports and I used to love watching T. Martin when he played football for the University of Tennessee. I loved the colors of their uniforms (I'm a girl, what can I say?) – hence the reason I named this slaw after them.

The Salad

3 cups jicama, peeled and shredded

3 cups carrots, shredded

1/3 cup golden raisins or soft dates, pitted and chopped

The Dressing

1/4 cup fresh lime juice

1/4 cup fresh orange juice

1 teaspoon fresh lime zest

1 teaspoon fresh orange zest

3 tablespoons raw agave nectar

1 teaspoon Himalayan crystal salt

1/4 teaspoon white pepper

Using a food processor, fitted with the shredding plate, shred the jicama and carrots. Transfer to a large bowl and add the raisins or dates.

Whisk the dressing ingredients together and pour over the salad ingredients. Gently toss.

If you're going to a party, then keep the salad mixture ingredients in a separate container from the dressing and combine them at the party just prior to serving.

SPROUT POWER MIX SALAD

Yield 2 - 3 servings

To learn how to easily grow your own sprouts, see my book, *Kristen's Raw: The EASY Way to Get Started & Succeed at the Raw Food Vegan Diet & Lifestyle* (available at KristensRaw.com) or visit my blog at:

www.kristensraw.blogspot.com/2008/04/this-is-how-i-sprout-easy-directions.html

The Salad

1 cup alfalfa or broccoli sprouts

1 cup sunflower sprouts

1 cup pea sprouts

1 cucumber, diced

2 medium tomatoes, diced

1/3 cup raisins

1/4 cup olives, pitted and chopped (any variety)

The Dressing

  1/2 cup raw tahini

  1/4 cup fresh lemon juice

  3 tablespoons water

  1 clove garlic

  1/4 teaspoon cumin

  1/2 teaspoon Himalayan crystal salt

  1/8 teaspoon black pepper

Assemble the salad ingredients in a large bowl (or on individual salad plates). Blend the dressing ingredients until creamy and pour the desired amount over the salad(s). If using a large bowl, then toss everything gently to mix well (otherwise, just drizzle the dressing on top of the plated salads and serve). Store any leftover salad dressing in an airtight container in the refrigerator for up to 5 days.

SUMMER PICNIC SLAW

See photo at KristensRaw.com/photos.

Yield 4 servings

Summer Picnic Slaw has so much to offer. It's filled with a rainbow of beautiful colors, and refreshing crunchy *and* creamy textures in every bite. You'll love it! Everyone does. In fact, people come up to me days after they've eaten it and tell me how much they loved it.

The Salad

1/2 head red cabbage, shredded

3 carrots, shredded

1 cucumber, peeled and diced

1 medium tomato, diced

3 scallions, thinly sliced

1/2 cup raisins

8 soft dates, pitted and chopped

1 tablespoon garlic, pressed

1 teaspoon Himalayan crystal salt

The Dressing

1/2 cup extra virgin olive oil or hemp oil

1/2 cup cashews, soaked 1 hour, drained and rinsed

1/3 cup water, additional if necessary for blending

1 tablespoon apple cider vinegar

1 1/2 tablespoons raw agave nectar

1/4 teaspoon cumin

1/4 teaspoon Himalayan crystal salt

dash cayenne pepper

Combine the salad ingredients in a bowl and toss to mix. For the dressing, place all of the ingredients in a blender, and blend until creamy. Pour the dressing over the salad and serve.

THE BEST CHOPPED SALAD EVER

Yield 2 servings

This salad is wonderful and sure to please everyone. It's full of crunchy, refreshing, and nutritious ingredients.

The Salad

1/2 head romaine lettuce, chopped

1/2 cup red bell pepper, destemmed, seeded and diced

1/2 cucumber, chopped

1/2 cup tomato, chopped

1/4 cup mango, peeled, seeded and diced (or more!)

6 kalamata olives, pitted and chopped

2 tablespoons fresh basil, minced

1 green onion, minced

1 tablespoon capers

The Dressing

3 tablespoons extra virgin olive oil

2 tablespoons water

2 tablespoons fresh lemon juice

1 teaspoon apple cider vinegar*

3/4 teaspoon raw agave nectar

1/2 teaspoon garlic, pressed

1/8 teaspoon Himalayan crystal salt, to taste

1/8 teaspoon onion powder

pinch cayenne pepper

pinch black pepper, to taste

Combine the ingredients for the salad in a large bowl. Blend all of the ingredients for the dressing until creamy. Add the dressing to the salad and toss to mix.

* If you don't have apple cider vinegar on hand, just substitute with lemon juice.

CRUNCHY WALNUT LEEK SALAD

Yield 2 - 3 servings

Nero believed that leeks would improve his singing voice. I might agree; I seem to be singing better these days. ☺

    3/4 cup walnuts, chopped
    1 leek, finely chopped*
    1/4 cup green olives, pitted and chopped
    1 head green leaf lettuce, torn into big leaves
    3 tablespoons fresh lime juice
    1/4 cup extra virgin olive oil
    1 teaspoon dried tarragon
    1/4 teaspoon Himalayan crystal salt (or more to taste)
    pinch black pepper, to taste

Combine the walnuts, leeks and olives and arrange on the lettuce leaves. Whisk the lime juice, extra virgin olive oil, tarragon, salt and black pepper and add just before serving.

* Dirt likes to hide in leeks, so make sure you wash well.

GRAPEFRUIT-JICAMA SALAD WITH CREAMY AVOCADO

See photo at KristensRaw.com/photos.

Yield 2 servings

The Salad Base

2 tablespoons raw agave nectar

2 tablespoons fresh lime juice (or lemon juice)

1 small jicama, peeled and julienne

2 red or pink grapefruit (or 3 oranges), peeled, white pith removed, and torn into segments

1/2 cup celery, chopped

Whisk together the agave nectar and lime juice, set aside. Toss the remaining ingredients in a bowl. Add the agave nectar mixture and toss to coat. Plate the salad mixture, reserving any leftover agave nectar mixture that is in the bowl.

The Creamy Avocado

Leftover agave nectar mixture (from the salad base)

1 avocado, pitted and peeled

2 tablespoons flax oil

1 tablespoon water (or more)

1/4 cup fresh lime juice

1/4 teaspoon Himalayan crystal salt, or more to taste

pinch black pepper, or more to taste

Blend all of the ingredients until smooth. Serve over the Grapefruit-Jicama Salad.

ZUCCHINI AND SQUASH LUNCH

Yield 2 servings

This is a very pretty, fresh, summertime salad.

2 (yellow) squash zucchini
2 (green) zucchini
1/4 cup extra virgin olive oil or hemp oil
2 - 3 tablespoons fresh lemon juice
2 tablespoons fresh basil, chopped
Himalayan crystal salt, to taste
black pepper, to taste

Chop the yellow squash into chunks. Using a mandoline or V-slicer, thinly slice the zucchini into rounds. Place the squash and zucchini in a bowl. Drizzle them with the olive oil and lemon juice. Add the basil, salt and pepper. Toss to mix and serve.

COLORFUL SPANISH CABBAGE SOIREE

Yield 3 - 4 servings

I love cabbage because it's so versatile. It's low in calories and contains folate, fiber, calcium and iron.

The Salad

2 cups green cabbage, shredded

1 cup red cabbage, shredded

1 cup carrots, shredded

1 cucumber, seeded and diced

1/2 cup sweet onions, chopped

1/2 cup corn, cut fresh from the cob, or frozen corn, thawed

The Dressing

1/2 cup extra virgin olive oil

2 tablespoons fresh lemon juice*

3 tablespoons fresh lime juice*

1 tablespoon raw agave nectar

1 teaspoon cumin

1 teaspoon chili powder, or Mexican seasoning

1/2 teaspoon paprika

1/2 teaspoon Himalayan crystal salt

1/4 teaspoon black pepper

Place the salad ingredients in a large bowl. Whisk the dressing ingredients together and pour over the salad.

* If you don't have both lemons and limes on hand, you can use 5 tablespoons of whichever one you have.

PARTHENON SALAD

Yield 3 - 4 servings

There are so many great flavors in this salad with all of the different vegetables. And, it's full of beautiful, vibrant colors, too.

The Salad

1/2 head romaine lettuce, chopped

4 medium tomatoes, cut into chunks

1 small jicama, peeled, julienne

1 orange bell pepper, destemmed, seeded and diced

2 green onions, thinly sliced

1/4 cup Greek or kalamata olives (or a mix of them), pitted and sliced

2 radishes, thinly sliced

2 tablespoons fresh mint, minced

The Dressing

1/4 cup extra virgin olive oil

2 tablespoons flax oil

1/4 cup fresh lemon juice

1/2 teaspoon fresh lime juice (substitute lemon if you don't have lime)

1/2 teaspoon dried oregano

1/2 teaspoon dried basil

1/2 teaspoon Himalayan crystal salt

black pepper, to taste

Combine the ingredients for the salad in a large bowl. Whisk together the ingredients for the dressing and pour onto the salad. Toss and serve immediately.

Note: if you're going to a party and want to bring this big delicious salad as your dish to pass, then bring the salad and dressing in separate containers and mix just before serving.

RAW FATTOUSH-FLAX CRACKER SALAD

Yield 4 servings

> 1 head romaine lettuce, chopped
>
> 1 cup parsley, chopped
>
> 1 red or orange bell pepper, destemmed, seeded and diced
>
> 1 cucumber, diced
>
> 3 medium tomatoes, chopped
>
> 4 radishes, thinly sliced
>
> 1 green onion, minced
>
> 1/3 small red onion, diced
>
> 4 - 5 flax crackers, broken into pieces
>
> 1 clove garlic, pressed
>
> 2/3 cup fresh lemon juice
>
> 1/3 cup extra virgin olive oil
>
> 2 tablespoons fresh oregano, chopped or 2 teaspoons dried
>
> 2 teaspoons sumac*
>
> 2 teaspoons dried mint or 1 tablespoon fresh mint, chopped
>
> 1/4 teaspoon Himalayan crystal salt

Place the lettuce, parsley, bell pepper, cucumber, tomatoes, radishes, green onions, red onion, and flax crackers in a large bowl.

In a small bowl whisk the garlic, lemon juice, olive oil, oregano, sumac, mint and salt together. Just before serving, pour the dressing on the salad and toss.

* You can find sumac at most Middle Eastern markets.

ORANGE RADISH SKY

Yield 2 - 3 servings

The Salad

2 bunches of radishes, washed and trimmed

2 oranges, peeled and chopped

The Dressing

1 1/2 tablespoons raw agave nectar

1 teaspoon orange flower water or filtered water

3 tablespoons extra virgin olive oil

1 1/2 tablespoons fresh lemon juice

2 tablespoons fresh orange juice

1/4 teaspoon Himalayan crystal salt (or more to taste)

Shred the radishes using a food processor, fitted with the shredding plate. Place the shredded radishes in small bowl and add the orange.

Whisk the ingredients for the dressing together. Pour this on top of the radishes and oranges. Stir and set aside for 15 minutes. Drain off excess liquid. Serve.

LIVING STYLE PEPERONATA

Yield 3 - 4 servings

I'm Italian, so I love the flavors of Italy and I eat them whenever I get the chance. Here is a great opportunity. ☺

1 small - medium red onion, thinly sliced

2 large zucchini, spiralized for angel hair pasta or peeled with a vegetable peeler like fettuccini

1 red bell pepper, destemmed, seeded, julienne

1 orange pepper, destemmed, seeded, julienne

1 yellow pepper, destemmed, seeded, julienne

2 tablespoons fresh basil, chopped or 2 teaspoons dried

1 tablespoon fresh oregano, chopped or 1 teaspoon dried

1 fresh sprig rosemary leaves, minced

1 tablespoon poppy seeds, optional

1/2 cup extra virgin olive oil

1/3 cup fresh lemon juice.

1/4 - 1/2 teaspoon Himalayan crystal salt (or more to taste)

pinch black pepper

Place all of the ingredients into a large bowl and toss. Enjoy.

DELICATE FENNEL SALAD

Yield 3 - 4 servings

Fennel is one of my favorite vegetables because it's sweet and crunchy. The whole plant is edible, from the bulb to the feathery leaves (you can cut the leaves and use them as an herb).

1/2 cup Raw mayonnaise of your choice (see recipes, pages 27 and 43)

2 tablespoons fresh lemon juice

1 1/2 tablespoons fresh dill, chopped

2 teaspoons raw agave nectar

1/2 teaspoon fresh lemon zest

1/4 teaspoon Himalayan crystal salt (or more to taste)

1/4 teaspoon black pepper (or more to taste)

2 large bulbs fennel, thinly sliced

1 orange or red bell pepper, destemmed, seeded and diced

1 - 2 oranges, peeled, seeded and chopped

Blend the Raw mayonnaise, lemon juice, dill, agave, lemon zest, salt, and pepper together. Trim the fennel and thinly slice the bulb with a mandoline or V-slicer. Toss the fennel, bell pepper, and orange with enough dressing to coat.

MY SPICY VEGETABLE TANGO

See photo at KristensRaw.com/photos.

Yield 2 - 3 servings

When I eat this slaw, I just want to get up and do the tango (yeah, and I don't even know how – go figure).

The Salad

2 large carrots, chopped

1 large yellow bell pepper, destemmed, seeded and chopped

1 large red bell pepper, destemmed, seeded and chopped

The Dressing

1/2 cup olive oil or hemp oil

1 1/2 tablespoons *Raw Mustard** (see recipe, p. 26)

2 Serrano red peppers, seeded and minced

2 teaspoons raw agave nectar

1/4 cup fresh lemon juice

1/4 teaspoon cayenne pepper

1 teaspoon freshly grated lemon zest

1/2 teaspoon cumin seeds

1/2 teaspoon celery seeds

1/2 teaspoon Himalayan crystal salt

1/4 teaspoon black pepper

Combine all of the salad ingredients in a bowl. Blend all of the dressing ingredients together. Pour over the salad. Toss it all together and enjoy.

* If you don't have *Raw Mustard* on hand or you don't have time to prepare it, then you can simply use store-bought mustard, even though it's not Raw.

APPLE CABBAGE SLAW

Yield 2 - 3 servings

This is a great slaw for serving at your next brunch.

The Salad

2 cups green cabbage, shredded

2 apples, cored and shredded

1 carrot, shredded

1 red bell pepper, destemmed, seeded and diced

2 tablespoons onion, minced

1 teaspoon dried dill

1/2 teaspoon Himalayan crystal salt

1/4 teaspoon black pepper

The Dressing

1/2 cup Raw mayonnaise of your choice (see recipes, pages 27 or 43)

1 tablespoon fresh lemon juice

1 tablespoon raw agave nectar

1 teaspoon onion powder

3/4 teaspoon cumin

1/4 - 1/2 teaspoon Himalayan crystal salt

pinch cayenne pepper

Combine the salad ingredients in a large bowl and toss. Blend together the dressing ingredients. Pour this over the salad mixture and toss well. Let stand at least 20 minutes in the refrigerator before serving.

Variations:

- Substitute 3/4 cup chopped celery for the red bell pepper
- Add 1/4 cup dried cranberries

"THE DEVIL MADE ME DO IT" SALAD

Yield 2 servings

The Salad

> 2 cups carrots, shredded
>
> 1/2 cup beets, shredded
>
> 2 oranges, peeled, seeded and chopped

The Dressing

> 1/4 cup water, more if needed
>
> 1 avocado, pitted and peeled
>
> 2 tablespoons fresh lemon juice
>
> 1 tablespoon fresh dill, chopped
>
> 1/2 teaspoon fresh ginger, grated
>
> 1/4 teaspoon powdered mustard
>
> 1/4 - 1/2 teaspoon Himalayan crystal salt (or more to taste)

In a salad bowl, combine the carrots, beets, and orange. Blend all of the dressing ingredients until smooth and creamy. Pour the dressing over the salad and toss to coat.

SUNRISE PINEAPPLE BREAKFAST SLAW

Yield 2 - 3 servings

This slaw is fun because you'll want to eat it for breakfast. Salad for breakfast? Heck yes!!!

- 1 small head green cabbage, shredded
- 2 apples, cored and shredded
- 1 pineapple, peeled, cored and chopped
- 1 cup pecans, coarsely chopped
- 2 tablespoons fresh lemon juice
- 1/4 teaspoon Himalayan crystal salt, optional

Combine all of the ingredients in a bowl. Toss to mix.

DAZZLING ITALIAN SHREDDED CABBAGE

Yield 3 - 4 servings

This is one of my step-dad's favorite salads. He's always asking me to bring it over.

The Salad

    1 head of green cabbage, shredded

    1/2 cup parsley, chopped

    2 green onions, chopped

    1/4 cup currants

    2 red bell peppers, destemmed, seeded and diced

    1/4 cup kalamata olives, pitted and chopped

    1/4 cup pine nuts

The Dressing

    1/4 cup fresh lemon juice

    1/2 cup extra virgin olive oil

    1 tablespoon raw agave nectar

    2 cloves garlic

    1 teaspoon dried basil

    1 teaspoon onion powder

    1/2 teaspoon dried oregano

    1/2 teaspoon Himalayan crystal salt

    1/8 teaspoon black pepper

Combine the salad ingredients in a large bowl and toss to mix. Blend the ingredients for the dressing together and pour over the cabbage mix. Toss to coat.

SUPER SPROUT-N-VEGGIE SALAD

Yield 4 servings

Sprouts should be a large part of anyone's life if they want optimal health. They're fun, extremely nutritious and can be added to just about anything!

4 cups spring lettuce mix

3 cups sprouts of your choice

1 red or yellow bell pepper, destemmed, seeded and diced

1 cucumber, diced

1 cup carrot, diced

1 zucchini, diced

2 stalks celery, chopped

1/4 cup currants, raisins, or dried cranberries

Divide all of the ingredients among four serving dishes (or two if you're looking for a huge salad to enjoy). Top with the dressing of your choice (see Chapter 2), and enjoy each bite of this truly amazing, phyto-nutrient-rich, energy-enhancing deliciousness.

KRISTEN SUZANNE'S PASSION SALAD

Yield 2 - 3 servings

This salad celebrates delicious passion, life, and excitement with each and every juicy bite!

2 oranges, juiced

2 limes, juiced

1 papaya, seeded, peeled and diced

(continued)

1 mango, peeled, pitted and diced

1/2 small pineapple, peeled, cored and chopped

1 kiwi, peeled and sliced

1 star fruit, thinly sliced

Put all of the ingredients into a gorgeous bowl and toss gently.

Breinigsville, PA USA
01 September 2009
223370BV00003B/83/P

9 780981 755663